W9-CAJ-734

Created and published by Knock Knock
1635-B Electric Avenue
Venice, CA 90291
knockknockstuff.com

Illustrations by Gemma Correll

ISBN: 978-160106626-8
UPC: 825703-50032-5

1 0 9 8 7 6 5

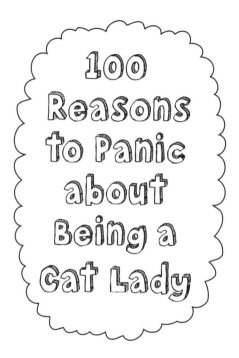

# 100 Reasons to Panic about Being a Cat Lady

KNOCK
KNOCK®
VENICE, CALIFORNIA

# 1.

# You'll show strangers photos of your cat.*

*It's payback for oohing and ahhing over all those baby photos.

# 2.

You'll give your cat silly nicknames like Professor Snugglepaws and Furry McFuzzerson.*

*He has nicknames for you, too.
They're not as cute.

**3.**

# You'll set up video feeds so you can watch your cat from work.*

*And then you'll finally know how
she fills her days.

# 4.

# Cats can't fill the emptiness inside.*

*Oh, wait. Yes, they can.

# Your cat is always staring at you.*

*Actually, he's judging you.

# 6.

# Your cat will pee on your stuff.*

*You probably needed to
replace those slippers anyway.

# 7.

# Your friends with allergies won't want to come over.*

**8.**

# How many cats is too many cats?*

**9.**

# You can't take a cat for a walk.*

*You won't have to wait while he pees on another bush, either.

# 10.

# You'll refer to your cat as your baby.*

*She *is* your baby—your fur baby.

# 11.

# People will start giving you cat mugs.*

*Wine + cat mug = classy!

# 12.

Your cat will
present you
with dead mice
as gifts.*

*Cats give you gifts.

# 13.

# Cats are aloof.*

*They prefer "discriminating."

# 14.

# Cats are sneaky.*

*They prefer "stealthy."

# 15.

## All your clothes will be covered in cat hair. *

*Is there a more perfect accessory for your
"I ♥ CATS" sweatshirt?

# 16.

You'll get weird and start making stuff out of "found" cat fur.*

*You're upcycling.

# 17.

# You'll never really understand your cat.*

*You'll never be bored by predictability.

# 18.

# A cat won't defend your home like a dog might.*

*Instead, a cat might break into your home.
Cats are crafty like that.

#

# You'll dress up your cat.*

*Where do you think the expression
"cat's pajamas" came from?

# 20.

# A cute kitten can turn into an ugly cat.*

*But she'll be your ugly cat.

**21.**

# All that leaping has you worried your cat will plunge to his death.*

*He has nine lives. Duh.

**22.**

# You'll start collecting cats.*

*They're cuter than comic books.

# 23.

# Purring is sort of creepy.*

*It's your cat's version of applause. The louder he purrs, the more adequate he considers you.

# 24.

# Cats hold grudges.*

*Easy solution: do not cross a cat.

# 25.

# You'll subscribe to Cat Fancy.*

*You can finally cancel those subscriptions to *Living Alone* and *Basketweaving Monthly*.

**26.**

# Your cat will constantly follow you around the house.*

# 27.

# Your cat will hog the bed.*

*Less sleep means more time to get things done.

# 28.

# You'll prefer hanging out with your cat.*

*Well, he *is* the best company.

# Cats have such an attitude.*

*They prefer "cattitude."

**30.**

# Your cat licks you— and you hate that feeling.*

# 31.

# You'll have to cat proof your home.*

*Don't bother—you can't outsmart a cat.

# 32.

# Hairballs are disgusting.*

*They camouflage dust bunnies quite well.

# 33.

# scratching posts
# are ugly.*

*You can start a line of
Eames-inspired cat accessories.

# 34.

# Your cat will end up addicted to catnip.*

*Cat twelve-step programs are a great place to make friends.

SIR FLUFFINGTON

**35.**

# You'll commission multiple portraits of your cat.*

*You'll be a patron of the arts.

# 36.

# You can't
# train a cat.*

*Being a drill sergeant is no fun, anyway.

# 37.

# Cats are born killers.*

*You'll have on-call pest control.

# 38.

# Cats are high-maintenance.*

*So are you.

# 39.

# Cats don't really do anything.*

*Finally, a living thing that doesn't want anything from you.

**40.**

# You'll throw birthday parties for your cat.*

*In return, he will give you the gift of tolerating your existence.

# 41.

# Your cat will meow constantly.*

*Those meows will drown out annoying car alarms, street noise, and loud neighbors.

# 42.

# Your cat will never ask about your day.*

*You won't have to listen to tedious stories about her day, either.

## 43.

# Your cat will escape, climb a tree, and never come down.*

HOME
SWEET
HOME

*You'll have to call a hunky firefighter
to rescue the cat.

**44.**

# You'll call yourself "cat mommy."*

---

# 45.

## Your cat has a cool literary name, and no one gets it.*

*You'll have a reason to expound upon the greatness of the classics.

# 46.

# Kitty litter is gross.*

*At least you won't have to take your cat out
at two in the morning when he's gotta go.

**47.**

# Your cat won't want to curl up with you on a rainy day.*

*That's called respecting your personal space.

**48.**

# Your toilet paper will end up shredded to bits.*

*But the joy it'll bring your cat will be priceless.

# 49.

## Your cat will hide under the bed for most of her waking hours.*

*You won't have to make
any awkward small talk.

# 50.

# Your home will smell like cat pee.*

*You'll have an excuse to buy fancy candles.
Lots of them.

**51.**

# You'll feel guilty leaving your cat alone all day.*

*Think of how excited she'll be when you return.
(She won't notice.)

# 52.

# You'll record a ton of cat videos.*

## 53.

# Your cat thinks everything is a toy created expressly for him.*

*Playing together relieves his stress—and yours.

**54.**

# Cat food is stinky.*

*That annoying guy at work who heats up fish
in the microwave will now make you feel
right at home.

## 55.

# You'll send holiday cards from you and your cat.*

*You'll have something to do with all the photos you take of her.

**56.**

# Your only conversation topic: your cat.*

# 57.

# You'll start to dislike dogs.*

*Dogs will love you regardless.

# 58.

# Your cat will
# be a bully.*

*You can put up a
"Beware of Cat" sign—and mean it.

# 59.

# Cats expect to be worshipped.*

*They come by it rightly; the cat goddess
Bastet inspired a cult in ancient Egypt.

**60.**

# Your new cat won't get along with your old cat.*

*But they might start fighting over your affection. Flattering!

# 61.

# Your cat
# will always demand
# your attention.*

*Someone needs you!

**62.**

# Your cat will always want to sleep in your freshly washed laundry.*

*When you wash your clothes again, they'll be extra-clean!

# 63.

# Vet visits are expensive.*

*You needed to get on a budget anyway.

**64.**

# You'll get carpal tunnel from petting your cat.*

# 65.

# Your cat will wake you up too early in the morning.*

*She's cuter than an alarm clock, isn't she?

# 66.

# You can't have just one cat.*

# 67.

# Your cat will get into your knitting projects.*

*His creativity will give you something to brag about.

**68.**

If you live with your sister and a bunch of cats, you might be dangerously close to Grey Gardens territory.*

*Maybe someone will make a documentary about you.

**69.**

# Your cat will only drink out of the sink.*

**70.**

# You'll never be able to find a cat-sitter you can trust.*

*Think of the money you'll save
when you only take staycations.

# 71.

# You'll get a tattoo of your cat.*

*In twenty years, you'll probably still like your cat. Can you say that about a butterfly?

# 72.

# Cats will scratch up your couch.*

*Covering it in plastic will make
it easier to wipe up spills.

# 73.

## When you want to order takeout, it's always sushi, sushi, sushi.*

*Your omega-3 levels will skyrocket.

**74.**

# Cat-owner stereotypes are not flattering.*

# 75.

## Your cat will only want to watch nature shows about avian species.*

*Birdwatching: your new shared hobby.

# 76.

# You'll never be alone.*

# 77.

# Your cat lacks ambition.*

*If you could spend your days
basking in the sun, wouldn't you?

# 78.

# Your cat will eat your plants.*

*She's trying to simplify your routines.

# You'll go broke investing in organic, chemical-free, preservative-free cat products.*

*At least one of you is eating well.

80.

# You'll dress exclusively in leopard and cheetah prints.*

*A signature look is a sign
of strong personal style.

# 81.

# It's hard to brush a cat.*

*But easier than brushing out the tangles
in a squirming toddler's hair.

# 82.

# Your cat will get sick every winter.*

*Is there anything cuter than a cat sneezing?

# 83.

# It's hard to clip
# a cat's claws.*

**84.**

# Your cat-less friends just don't understand how hard it is to raise cats.*

*They also don't understand
unconditional love, the poor things.

## 85.

# All those cats will scare off potential suitors.*

**86.**

# Having a cat is less social than having a dog.*

*It's a perfect excuse to stay in your pajamas and watch movies all day.

# You'll always be vacuuming up fur.*

*You'll be able to eat off your floors.

# 88.

# You'll never
# please your cat.*

*You won't. But your efforts will entertain him.

# 89.

## Your cat will never shut up.*

*And you'll learn another language: Cat.

**90.**

# Whenever you're reading the newspaper, your cat wants to sit on top of it.*

*Goodbye gloom and doom—
hello, sweet furry face!

## 91.

# Your cat will eat all of your fancy cheese.*

*Teaching him to diet will
prepare him for cat pageants.

# All your hard-earned money will go to cat toys.*

*Your cat will be most excited about the empty boxes.

## 93.

# The paw-kneading across your body will get annoying.*

*Daily massages sound kind of nice.

# Cat scratches hurt.*

*Better your arms than your couch.

# 95.

## Your cat's not as talented as the cats you see on the Internet.*

*Neither of you will have to deal with the pressures of fame.

# 96.

# You'll start taking in feral cats.*

*You can get nonprofit status as a wildlife refuge.

# 97.

# what if the world ends and it's just you and your cat?*

*Cats are excellent hunters. You'll never starve.

# 98.

# Dog people act superior.*

*Is there a more codependent animal than the slobbery hound?

# 99.

# Cat ladies aren't sexy.*

I ♥ CATS

*What about Catwoman?

# 100.

You won't be able to relate to non-cat people.*

*Why bother?